The Connecticut Common School Journal
V13, May, 1866: And Annals Of Education

Board Of Commissioners Common Schools

In the interest of creating a more extensive selection of rare historical book reprints, we have chosen to reproduce this title even though it may possibly have occasional imperfections such as missing and blurred pages, missing text, poor pictures, markings, dark backgrounds and other reproduction issues beyond our control. Because this work is culturally important, we have made it available as a part of our commitment to protecting, preserving and promoting the world's literature. Thank you for your understanding.

THE
Connecticut Common School Journal

AND

ANNALS OF EDUCATION.

Vol. XIII.	NEW BRITAIN, MAY, 1866.	No. 5.

CULTIVATION OF TASTE.
BY PROF. LOUIS BAIL, YALE COLLEGE.

THE immense sums of money continually expended in our cities in building, and the general absence of architectural taste displayed by builders, form a deplorable and disproportionate contrast; in proof of this, you have only to visit our crowded business marts, or those portions of our cities devoted to private aristocratic dwellings; the eye is continually pained by the sight of immense piles of stone, stucco or of——

> "bricks,
> Where all the orders in disorder mix."

Heavy window-dressings and balconies, resting on—— nothing; porticoes that look as if borrowed from neighbors' dwellings, and placed against other walls as a temporary convenience; Egyptian cornices frowning over Corinthian capitals, crowning a Doric column, the whole shading a row of painted Gothic windows; with every conceivable and inconceivable inharmonious combination, that can arise from ignorance of true architectural taste. There is not sufficient unity in the form and decorations of our buildings; to the cultivated eye, the parts of such a building form as disproportionate a contrast as would a female figure arrayed in a Parisian bonnet, flowing with snow-drops and violets, a cashmere shawl, with seal skin Esquimaux small clothes, and moccasins.

With the immense expenditure of money upon both public edifices and private dwellings, an expenditure at present unequaled by any other nation, this surely ought not to be; our buildings should be as pre-eminent in architectural beauty, as they are in luxurious magnificence, and as are our steamboats, yachts and pilot boats, in symmetry of form, and adaptation of purpose.

It can not be believed that there is in America a scarcity of good architects, and we are compelled to conclude that this deformity in building arises from the ignorance and indifference of business men to fine arts and to those principles upon which alone true symmetry and beauty in building are produced. Never was a greater mistake made by men of business, than this continued tendency to shut themselves away from interest in the fine arts, and from intercourse with those who have a practical and scientific knowledge of them.

The perception of beauty is one of the high privileges of the human mind; it is the language of the eye, and, like speech, distinguishes man from the animal.

The operation of the mind whereby the judgment comprehends, compares, and finally adopts impressions of approvals, or dislike, is expressed by the term, taste: within its range is included an estimation of the moral and physical qualities of objects,—its decisions give intelligence to the senses, and zest to the feelings; thus are individual habits and pursuits formed; and implied in one sentence, the taste is the man.

Ornamental taste is excited and gratified by contemplation of the beautiful, and exists independently of higher aspirations, for that which presents to the senses harmony of arrangement, and fitness of purpose, whether it refers to the

Cultivation of Taste. 131

beautiful in nature, or the productions of human ingenuity, is alike an object of interest to the refinement induced by a good system of education, and is singled out, as assimilating with the impressions of a highly cultivated imagination.

The elements of taste are portions of a common inheritance; simple in themselves, they are capable of that infinite variety of combination with stronger powers of mind, which, combined, exhibit degrees of this faculty remarkably diverse. The informed perception and tastes to a certain extent attend each other; at this point commences the light and shade of opinion, and character,—the similarities that unite, or the antipathies that repel.

It is evident that taste is most successfully cultivated where the perceptive faculties are earliest directed to examples and models upon which a good taste may be founded. It is also evident the taste may be soon perverted by bad examples and models.

Examples of art and practical lessons concerning these examples are the best means of the development of the perceptions towards the attainment of the ornamental arts, and are subjects of great interest to all concerned in the advance of these arts.

We can never be correct in any study till we are well grounded in its elements; when we are incorrect in these we must fail in our after deductions. Examples of art, to produce a general effect upon the masses, must be accompanied by sound elementary instruction; especially must he who desires to apply these arts to useful and ornamental purposes receive these instructions. The purity and susceptibility of the earlier stages of perception, before taste has become vitiated by bad examples in art, justly demand at our hands the highest impressions of truth and beauty.

The foundation for the cultivation of taste should be laid in our common schools by suitable elementary instruction in drawing.

I believe the day is not far distant when a school of design will be established in this State; but great results can not be expected from such an Institution until the pupils receive the first elements of drawing in all our common schools and in this way prepare the material for a school of design. My own experience as a teacher enables me to bear testimony that the capacity and talents of the people in this State warrant the establishment of a school of design here.

Though sadly perverted and misapprehended, drawing is now universally considered an essential part of a good education, some knowledge of which is sought by every person laying claim to good taste; it is of great value as a means of refinement and culture; also as an aid to pleasure and happiness.

A knowledge of drawing, and especially of the rules of perspective, forms an intelligent and correct observer of nature. The ability to sketch from nature affords very great happiness. It is a great advantage to the traveller,—preserving fresh, scenes that would otherwise grow dim in the lapse of time; and no psychological work will give such ready and correct knowledge of human character, such power of reading the soul at a glance, as is obtained by the artistic study of the human head and face.

Parents are much to blame for the defects in our drawing system. They seem unwilling to wait for results as in other studies. It is deeply to be regretted, that people do not bring the same amount of common sense to bear upon this department of culture, that they do upon every other. You wisely mistrust any system that promises great results with little labor in any other department of knowledge. I believe there is no study that has primarily been placed in the hands of such an unmitigated set of bunglers as drawing. An unbroken and untrodden field would be easier for the true teacher than he usually finds.

Ornament is the pleasing and proper embellishment of surface, and is susceptible of adding much grace, beauty and delicacy to the object adorned. And let us not scorn ornament as a valueless thing; taking an example from God's created objects, we find outward adornment every where; this principle is founded in a universal law of nature, where nothing is bare and blank, but all is infinitely varied with ornaments indicative of character. God seems to delight in making the outer world in its minutest parts beautiful to our eyes—and the microscope reveals numberless beauties hidden from our unaided vision. Cowper says:

> " Not a flower
> But shows some touch in freckle, streak, or stain,
> Of his unrivaled pencil."

The simplest form of embellishment is the spot, or point; delicately distributed or clustered in brilliant groups, it is the most simple mode of embellishment; it gives lustre to the eye, beautifies the fish that glides beneath the silver wave, diversifies the fur of the leopard tribe, and the wing of the pheasant, and many other of feathered creation; gives variety even to the creeping reptile, and tiny insect; the eggs of birds, the seeds of plants; and different kinds of marble are decorated in this simple manner; many kinds of flowers, wood and leaves are ornamented in the same way. The stars twinkling in a clear field of blue, afford a striking illustration of the beauty produced by the use of the dot.

The line occurs next in the order of definitions, though it undoubtedly occupies the first place in ornamental arrangements of every kind. The straight line is more properly the line of structure than of ornament; the far-off horizon at sunrise and sunset is a fine illustration of the beauty of this line; before day dawn all nature lies in quiet shade, but at that moment she starts from her repose, awakened by a streak of light; so on, another and another follow; lines rise and diverge till day is ushered in. The Aurora is a similar illustration.

Lines of a varied or curvilinear character are essentially those of beauty. This line predominates wherever grace or beauty exists. The rainbow is the most splendid illustration of the grace of a simple curve.

Form is itself ornamental, if ease, dignity and elegance are secured, but when in addition to this, the surface is most appropriately embellished with ornamental designs, it will approach nearest to perfection. To obtain both these excellencies we must study and apply the curve line.

The action of the wind upon the clouds and waves produces remarkable examples of the power of lines to express character. The most agreable objects in nature or art derive their beauty from some peculiarity of the curve line in their formation. Indeed the existence of this line seems to endow an object with grace. The artist and the designer behold every where in nature, on earth, in sea, or floating in the sky, models for study. If he designs an awkward or ungraceful thing, he shuts his eye upon the teachings of nature which are ever spread out before him and drawn in lines so plain "that he who sees may read." Out of a few simple elements the artist works wondrous combinations in the field of art. He takes his first lesson from the globe; which, as it possesses immutable proportions, represents truth. In this he must also be immutable and unchanging. Every object must be just as it appears to be. He takes his second from the pyramid, which represents strength; it stands firm and immovable amid the storms of the desert—yet it is susceptible of change without loss of strength; last, from the ellipseoid, the example of grace. While the true artist never sacrifices truth to beauty, he makes the very best use of the material he has to work upon. While he never yields strength to grace—he clothes the angular frame with the soft flowing lines of beauty. So works he, that out of sameness comes variety,—out of plainness, beauty.

For the Common School Journal.
KNOW YOUR SCHOLARS.

Every young person, entering upon the labors of a schoolroom, has very indistinct ideas of the duties he is called t perform. Perhaps every such one has a crude theory, floating shapeless in the brain-world, which he expects to reduce to practice. He hears constantly of the difficulty of government, and the necessity of firmness and self-command: and there rises before him, in visions of anticipation, some obstinate pupil, resisting his mild sway, and infusing rebellion in the heart of the school. He—the teacher—summons all his strength, and calmly stands, a monument of self-possession, pronounces sentence upon the unlucky offender, and subdues his entire charge by one awful glance. So that matter is disposed of, and the good ship government sails in calm seas again.

Now any one who has worked in a school-room knows that this is all nonsense. So far as my own observation goes there is very seldom a severe case of discipline:—an instance of willful resistance, or prolonged obstinacy, and these cases which can be severely dealt with, are most easily managed of all. It is the repeated thoughtlessness, the indolent, restless, or fun-loving propensity, that is constantly presenting trial and perplexity before the teacher. There is real satisfaction in conquering a "hard case;" but there is tormenting worry and weariness in the thousand petty annoyances, which occur every day in a school-room, and which a young, and sometimes an old teacher, often finds it hard to meet, and do away.

Here was my trouble in my first year of teaching. Mary would giggle, Julia would fuss, Jimmie would do things to make the boys laugh; and many of these things would be done in such a way as to avoid an actual infringement on any school regulation. Knowing nothing of my scholars except what I had seen in school, I was puzzled how to take hold of things, yet felt that they must be checked immediately. I decided to punish severely every thing that could in any way be interpreted as disobedience, and thus take in many offences which had hitherto called forth only slight reproof, and were becoming great annoyances, and hindering the smooth working of the school.

With this resolution, I entered the school-room one bright Monday morning. Monday is always a hard day in school. As a bright little fellow said to me once: "We just get a going by Friday, and then Saturday and Sunday push us off the track again." The morning passed off very well, but in the afternoon I caught Martha C. in the act of whispering. It was not her first offence of that nature, and being a direct infringement of a school rule, I felt that it must not be passed by; I would make her an example, both for her own punishment, and to save further trouble.

Of the child I knew next to nothing. She had not been a very regular attendant at school, and the soiled slip of paper she brought me occasionally, with the words: "Please excuse Martha for absence yesterday," gave little insight of her nature or life.

Still I hesitated what course to take. I looked at the child. She was about eleven years old, and rather above common height. A white face; pale eyes that always looked fixed and dead; a kind of drooping, quivering mouth; thin, nervous hands. These were all I saw. I spoke to her suddenly.

"Were you whispering, Martha?"

"Yes ma'am."

"Don't you know that whispering is forbidden?"

"Yes ma'am."

"You may go up stairs to Mr. D."

The child looked round wildly; then giving a nervous start she left the room, and I continued the recitations. Already I saw the effect of my severity. The scholars looked in my face, but it answered them nothing. The room became still, and bright faces assumed a subdued expression. I thought it promised well, but it pained me. I had been in the habit of dealing with trifling offences myself, and only sending the most serious ones to the principal, and I knew the offender must suffer—perhaps was already suffering. My feelings were very acute, and now and then I listened. All was still. No dull sound of blows was heard—no wailing cry.

An hour passed. How quiet my room seemed. I was glad to hear the primary scholars in the yard, and send mine to join them. Martha had not returned. I began to make inquiries for her, and what was my surprise and indignation when I learned that she had not been to the principal at all, and was nowhere to be found. Search was made and she was discovered in an ante-room in another part of the building.

They led her to me, and I felt no sympathy for her fright, but I did not lose my temper.

"Why did not you go up stairs, Martha?" I asked.

"I did ma'am," she answered: not coolly, not deliberately, for every nerve was strained and quivering.

"You have added untruth to disobedience," said I, "and it will be the worse for you. I shall myself go with you to Mr. D., as you can not be trusted alone, and tell him your double fault."

As I arose, she broke into a wild, impetuous pleading.

"Don't send me up stairs. I am sick. I can't be whipped. Oh, I'll niver do it again; indade I niver will. I'll be a good child, I will; only don't send me up the stairs, don't; it will kill me. I shall die; oh, I am so sick. Just try me this once, and see how good I will be!"

And by these words I first knew that Martha was an Irish child. Her entreaties were unheeded. I took her hand firmly in mine, and led her up stairs. She walked reluctantly at my side, still pleading, till we had reached the second landing; then screaming "O my heart!" she fell heavily across my arm. I lifted and carried her—a dead weight—up the remaining stairs, and placing her in the arms of a sister teacher, I ran for restoratives. We dashed water in her face, and poured it down her neck and back. It was as if she had been stone. There she lay, cold and senseless; her head drooping, her jaw fallen, her pale eyes fixed and glassy, her fluttering heart *so still.* We chafed her cold hands, but it gave them no warmth. Would she never revive? We sent for hartshorn, but it was a long time before she was restored by its application. Then she started suddenly. Her first glance fell on Mr. D., and she screamed. He spoke kindly to her. "No one shall hurt you, Martha." She looked at me as much as to say, "You have not told him yet." Then as she seemed excited by his presence, I carried her back to my room. She was lying passive in my arms, when I heard an eager voice, and a large, muscular woman came in. I needed no one to tell me who she was. There was all *the mother* in her voice.

"Where is my Martha; my child, my own little Martha?"

I answered her quietly, and one of my scholars gave her a chair by me.

"Spake to me, Martha, my poor, dear child! Were you hurt, Martha? Did the misthress be hard wi' ye? O, my poor child! Spake one word to your mother!"

Then she turned to me:

"They came to me—that boy, and the one yonder—and said the master was about to whip my girl, and she *died*; and I left the house and my clothes in the tub, and niver stopped running till I came inside this."

I told her briefly the story; neither attempting to justify the child or myself. I felt bitterly that both were wrong, but she least so. I had heard how "unreasonable" the Irish were, and expected vehement reproaches. I think I could have borne them better than what I did get, for she said:

"Indade you did quite right, Miss, and Martha was a bad child and deserved it all; but if ye's had known about her, perhaps ye would not have sent her to the master. You see she had the scarlet fever, four years ago, and she has niver been the same since. She ates nothin' at all for breakfast, and only a bite at other times. You might have noticed her to be a bit dafe, and she does not remember anything just rightly, and she always has that absent kind of a look, and starts as if she was away off when ye spake her name, and at times her heart beats and flutters like it was bigger nor the place that holds it, and the doctor says she has it bad, and must hear only soft words, or a fright will be the end of her. But I forget the same meself now and then, and only last wake, she broke the glass, and I said at dinner the father would be sure to whip her, and when she heard his step, she was just like dead, and she with the spoon in her mouth, so sudden like. Then she was sick with the heart of her for two days, and the father said it wouldn't be him as would ever strike her another blow, for she is indade a good child mostly. See she is asleep now, but for fear of the heart I'd be afther takin' her home wi' me till I finish the wash."

So she took the child in her stout arms and left me. I did not see Martha for a week afterward. She was "sick with the heart of her" again. Poor thing! She came back to school a trifle paler and thinner, and the little she had learned —for she was a dull scholar—was forgotten. I did not mention the punishment again, and it may have seemed like a fearful dream to her. I hope she did not think it real. She left me soon after when the Catholic school was established, but when I met her she always gave a glad start, and smiled up into my face, as if I had not sinned against her.

I knew where the wrong was. It was in not studying the physical, as well as mental capacities of my pupils. I ought to have heard that honest Irish mother's story long before, and dealt gently with her frail child, instead of choosing her to suffer as an example for the school. As for the punishment of her own fault, it might easily have been managed some other way. She was not willfully disobedient, or naughty, and who knows but by better knowledge, she might have been taught a lesson which should counteract many an evil influence in her after life.

My second school was composed of scholars with whom I had been familiar from their infancy, and I hope I did them no wrong; but were I to enter another school of strangers, I would endeavor to be personally acquainted with the homes and friends of my pupils: to know their habits and peculiarities, their physical temperaments and powers; so to deal rightly with them, that I may never again hear the reproachful words, "*If you had only known!*" with reference to what it is not only my privilege, but bounden duty to know.

Children are not like marbles: all rounded and smoothed in one mould. Each one has its peculiar trait and besetment. We can not have a fixed method for all. The skillful physician does not treat fever and rheumatism alike because both are disease. No more can we deal alike with different dispositions and tempers because all are faulty. Nourishment for one is poison for another. But each has his vulnerable point. In one way or another you may find access to every heart, and gain an influence which shall render control easy and pleasant. Study these ways and means. Enter in at the door; for he that "climbeth up some some other way, the same is a thief and a robber." God save him from being a murderer too.　　　BEULAH B.

March 28th, 1866.

PHONIC READING.
SECOND STEP.

THE words to which the children are introduced in this step are arranged in the following classes: 1st. Silent letters: 2d. Long sounds of the vowels, together with a few words, which are to be learned at sight, containing different sounds of the vowels; 3d. The sounds of *k, q*, and the two sounds of *c* and *s;* 4th. Two initial consonants; 5th. Two terminal consonants; 6th. Three initial consonants; 7th. Silent initial consonants; 8th. Central silent consonants; 9th. Terminal silent consonants; 10th. Central silent vowels; 11th. Terminal silent *e;* 12th. Terminal silent *ue*.

At the commencement of the second year the children may be introduced to reading books, such as are ordinarily used in this grade, and the subject-matter of the second and third steps is treated as a spelling-lesson.

1st. Silent Letters.—Let the teacher write upon the board a number of words containing silent letters, such as *bill, fill, hill, dick, stick, high, sigh*, etc. Let the children spell the word *bill* by sound several times, and let them give each sound separately. Ask, "How many sounds are there in this word?" "How many letters?" and lead them to say that it has four letters, and but three sounds. Ask the children, "What can you say about one of these letters?" and they will say, "It has no sound." Let them point out the letter that has no sound. The teacher may then tell them that those letters in a word which are not sounded, are called *silent letters.*

Exercise the class thoroughly on the term *silent*. Proceed in the same way with at least one of each of the class of words upon the board. Let the children cross out all the silent letters in each.

In a similar manner let several lessons be given, the teacher calling upon the class to give words with silent letters, which they may have had in their reading lessons, or names of common things with which they are familiar and can spell readily. In all cases, the child giving the word should spell it, the teacher printing it upon the board, and then calling upon the class to spell it in concert. At the close of the lesson the work must be erased from the board and the class required to reproduce it upon their slates, and this should be done with all Second and Third Step lessons.

2d. *Long vowel sounds.*—Let the teacher write the word *mad* upon the board. Let the children spell it by sound, and give each sound separately, dwelling particularly on the vowel sound, the teacher calling for the first sound in the word, the second, etc., thus avoiding the term *vowel*, which should not be used with the children. To the right of it write *made*, and treat it in the same way. Let them give the two vowel sounds separately several times. Ask, "What difference do you observe in these two sounds?" and they will say, "one sounds longer than the other." "What name then shall we give to these sounds?" The children will probably say, "long and short," but if they do not, the teacher may give the terms. The class may then be called upon to give numerous examples of words containing these sounds, the children spelling the words and the teacher printing them upon the board. Proceed in a similar manner with each of the other vowels. One vowel will be sufficient for a lesson.

In all of these exercises the teacher should prepare a list of words suitable to the children, which she can suggest in case they fail to furnish the required number of examples. A word should never be told a child until it has been first suggested, and the idea properly developed. One of the most important of Pestalozzian principles is, "Develop the idea; then give the term."

The children may at first be inclined to give non-significant words, but these should be rejected, and they should be encouraged to give only significant words.

After a sufficient number of words has been obtained and put upon the board, let the pupils go over the whole list, spell each word by sound and by letter, give the meaning of the words, and form statements containing each word. A little conversation may be had about such words as are particularly suggestive, but not so much as to lose sight of the object of the lesson.

In a similar manner all future lessons in this subject should be given.

3d. *Sounds of k and q.*—Place the letter *k* upon the board; give the sound, and ask the children if they have ever heard this sound before, and if they can find a letter upon the large card which has this sound. Suggest to the children a number of words commencing with this sound, as *cap, can, kill, kind,* etc., and place them upon the board in opposite columns. Let the class spell and pronounce the two lists, and give the sound of each, especially the first sound in each word. Ask what difference they observe in these words, and lead them by questions to see that they all commence with the same sound, but with different letters. Let them give a further list of words with *k*, as *hark, bark, sink, kick*, etc., and proceed as in previous lessons.

In a similar manner the letter *q* may be treated.

Hard and soft sounds of c.—The teacher may suggest to the class such words as *cedar, cell, cinder, cat, cut, cold,* etc. Place them upon the board, and let the pupils spell and pronounce each word, give each sound separately, and dwell particularly on the first sound. Lead them to compare these first sounds, by requiring them to give them in succession, and ask, "What difference do you observe in these sounds?" The class will perhaps say, that "one has a soft sound" and "the other a hard sound." If they do not, the teacher may now give the terms *hard* and *soft*. Lead them to see that the hard sound is like *k*, and the soft sound like *s*. Call on the children to give more examples, suggesting, if they fail to give them promptly, and proceed according to previous directions. The two sounds of *s, u* sounded as *w, n* as *ng*, and *y* as *i* long, may now be treated in the same way.

4th. Double initials.—Let the teacher suggest a few such words as *black, blanket, blind,* etc., by asking what we put over us at night that is made of wool; and what we say of a person who can not see, etc. The teacher prints the words, and causes the children to spell them by sound and by letter. Let them give the first sound in each word separately. (The two consonants *b* and *l* are sounded together.) Tell the class that the first sound in a word is called *initial* sound. Exercise them thoroughly on this term. The teacher may then ask, "How many letters form this sound?" "If two letters form this sound, what kind of an initial sound would you say it is?" If the pupils fail to say *double initial,* refer them to soldiers marching singly and two abreast, and obtain from them the term *double file.* They will then immediately give the term *double initial.* Then ask, "What letters form this double initial?" and place above the column on the board the words, "*Bl initial,*" and require the children to give words commencing with this sound, and proceed as in previous lessons.

The double initial consonants are *bl. sc, sk, br, cl, cr, dr, dw, fl, fr, pl, pr, sl, sm, sn, sp, st, sw, tr, tw,* and *qu.* Examples,—*black, scum, skim, brick, clod, crib, drop, dwell, flock, frock, plum, press, slip, smell, snap, split, step, swing, tramp, twist, quill.*

The term *consonant* must not be given to the children, but they should be merely called double initial sounds.

One sound is sufficient for a lesson, and a long list of words should be obtained from the children under each head, and treated after the foregoing models.

5th. Two terminal consonants.—Suggest such words as *told, hold, gold,* etc., and direct the attention of the class to the last two sounds, and develop the term *double terminal* in the same way as the term *double initial.* The children exercised as before; lists made out, etc.

The double terminal consonants are *lb, ld, nd, ff, lf, ck, lk, nk, sk. ll, lm, sm, lp, mp, sp, ct, st, ft, ng, lt. nt, rl, ss.* and *rf,*

Examples,—*Bulb, held, wind, cliff, self, brick, silk, ink, mask, drill, elm, prism, help, stamp, lisp, act, lost, drift, sling, melt, went, curl, muss, turf.*

6th. *Three initial consonants.*—These may be developed and treated in the same way as *two initial consonants.* They are *scr, spr, str, spl, squ.* Ex.—*Scrap, spry, string, splint, squint.*

7th. *Silent initial consonants.*—These may be developed in the same manner as silent letters, and the children will give the term *silent initial.* They are *g, h, k, p, w.* Ex.—*Gnat, herb, knife, psalm, whole, write.*

8th. *Central silent consonants.*—The term *central silent* may be drawn from the children in a manner similar to the other terms, by asking the children what they say of any thing that is in the middle. Words should first be suggested and put upon the board, and the lesson treated as the others. They are *b, c, d, g, h, gh, l, p, t, w,* and *s.* Ex.—*Debt, scene, scissors, lodge, handsome, sign, ghost, rhomb, isthmus, school, light, talk, calm, tempt, castle, pitch, sword, isle.*

9th. The *terminal silent consonants* are *b, k, gh,* and *h.* Ex.—*Lamb, wick, plough, Sarah.*

10th.—The *central silent vowels* are *e, i,* and *u.* Ex.—*Open, carriage, guilt.*

11th.—*Terminal silent e—ce, ble, cle, dle,* and *fle.* Ex.—*Nice, fable, uncle, handle, ruffle.*

12th.—The examples of *terminal silent ue* are *league, tongue,* etc.

The classification of sounds into those having *a tone*, and those having *no tone*, must be continued throughout this Step, as it prepares the way for the classification of sounds into tonics, subtonics, and atonics, which is done in the Third Step.—*Mich. Teacher.*

DOCTRINE OF THE TYPICAL FLOWER.

BY PROF. WOOD.

It is not possible to study the structure of the flower successfully; that is, to obtain any good understanding of that structure, without a constant reference of the design to the Designer. Let us therefore approach and view our theme in a divine light, as the creation of a Creator, the idea of a Deity. For, considered as a fortuitous result of chance, all the exquisite forms and marvelous adaptations of vegetable life become dreams and absurdities; but when considered as expressions of a divine idea, the flower, with all its splendor of adornment and its wondrous contrivances, stands forth as a most eloquent teacher of humanity.

Next to their beauty, one of the first things which excites admiration in viewing the world of flowers, is their variety. This seems to be infinite. In color, flowers vary to endless shades and hues; in form, to an extent which seems to the casual observer utter confusion; in size, to every conceivable degree from the microscopic to the monstrous; in season, also, in duration, in hardihood, texture, and perfume, they are also equally various. And yet, notwithstanding all this diversity, the flower is still a *flower*. There is discernible even in the extremest disguises, an ever-present principle or idea, whatever it be, which announces both to the learned and the unlearned, the presence of a flower. But what is that principle or idea? What is the one thing which in the flower remains constant, while everything else about it may be changed? In short, what is the original and completed idea, stripped of all its irregularities and disguises? This is the question which science asks and answers.

Stated in its true, that is, in its *sacred* import, the question is: "What was or is that prime conception which first existed in the infinite mind of God when He determined to create the flower—the idea which He now embodies in those glorious objects, and through them now offers to us for the instruction and elevation of our own minds?" That conception, although embodied in forms so various, is in itself perfectly simple and definite, containing the germs of a boundless diversity, and equally capable of harmonizing all extremes in itself. Such a conception *there is*, and it exists independent of any material embodiment, just as we may *now* affirm the existence of the Lily, while every plant of that kind lies dormant or dead under the frosty rigor of winter.

It is perfectly in order to search out this *beau ideal* of the floral structure, now called in scientific phrase, *the typical flower*. In that, *if attained*, we shall possess one of the thoughts of the Deity!—and it will be to us as a key wherewith to interpret the meaning of the strangest of the fantastic forms into which the flowers diverge. Without the knowledge of this type, any adequate understanding of the floral structure is impossible.

The first characteristic of the typical flower is thus stated. Four classes of organs, each class distinctly differing from the other three, and arranged circularly, constituting four concentric circles.

The second characteristic is thus announced. Let the number of organs constituting each of the four classes be the same in all. For example: If there be three sepals in the calyx, there should be three petals in the corolla, three stamens in the third circle, and three styles in the fourth or inner circle; or, if there be five pieces in the outer circle, there must be five in all.

The third characteristic of the typical flower is this: Let the several organs of each circle be alternate in position with the organs of the adjacent circles. In other words, the sepals must be alternate with (not opposite to) the petals; the petals must be alternate with the sepals, and with the stamens, and so on.

The fourth postulate is, that each and every organ of the type be free and distinct; that is, there must be no cohesions nor adhesions among them. The sepals must be *distinct* from each other and *free* from the petals, stamens, or styles; the petals must stand distinct from each other, and free from the sepals, stamens, etc.

The fifth and final. Let the several organs in each circle be similar and uniform in all respects; that is, similar in form, size, and position. The sepals must all be alike among themselves; the petals also, the stamens, and the styles. In consequence of this, the type is uniform on all sides, neither cramped nor oblique. In a word, it is *regular*.

The structure of the typical flower, as above described, will become still more apparent if epitomized as follows.

1. It is a *quaternion*—having four sets of organs arranged in four concentric circles.

2. It is *symmetrical*—having the same number of organs in each circle.

3. It is *alternated*—having the several organs of each circle alternate in position with the adjacent organs.

4 It is *regular*—having the several members of any one of the circles, in all respects alike.

5 It is *absolute*—having each and every organ distinct and uncombined.

Such is the type, the completed flower; but we must search long before we find it *perfectly* illustrated in nature. Among a myriad of species, not one may be found exactly conformable; and still, not one shall be found without an evident *tendency* in that direction. Hence that infinite variety and that apparent independence of set forms which characterize the flowers and impart to them an interest which is ever new.

In conclusion, we add a few illustrations showing how the endless diversity in the floral world may be consistent with this unity of plan, and how the former results not from the violation of the latter, but from sportive modifications of it.

The genus Crassula (natives of Africa) gives us perfect examples of the type, having five sepals, five petals, five stamens, and five styles—all uniform, all distinct, all alternate. The Flax (*Linum*) approaches very near, deviating only in having the five styles united below into one ovary. The Tulip deviates a little further, having its three styles completely united, and a double quota (six) of stamens.

Again, there are flowers deficient in one or more of the four circles of organs. For example: Anemone has no corolla. The flowers of Ash have neither calyx nor corolla. Begonia develops a part of her flowers without stamens, and the rest without pistils. The flowers of Snowball have neither stamens nor pistils. Such deficiencies are very numerous. Some flowers develop a redundancy of organs. The Rose has its stamens increased to forty or fifty, in eight or ten circles. The Lily has two circles of stamens. Magnolia has two or three circles of petals. Buttercups thus multiply both their stamens and pistils, always to some multiple of five, acknowledging always the law of circles.

Secondly. The flower may be deficient in only a part of some circle. Thus the Balm (Monarda) develops only two stamens of her five. She attempted, however, to develop the other three, as may be seen on inspection. The Larkspur produces only three or four of her quota of her petals; Aconite but two (the other three may be found by searching). Such exceptions only confirm the rule.

Thirdly. The flower may vary in its *radical number*, which we may suppose to be normally five. Thus in the Lily, three is the radical number (three sepals, three petals, three stamens, repeated, three pistils); in Syringa, four; in Berberry, six; and in Houseleek, twelve.

Fourthly. The flower may deviate from the *regularity* of the type, becoming oblique or one-sided, as seen in the Petunia but slightly, and in the Sages excessively.

Again, there are endless deviations in respect to cohesions and adhesions. Witness the Morning Glory, whose five petals are completely united, edge to edge, into a single funnel-shaped piece; the Pink, whose sepals are similarly conjoined; the Phlox, whose petals are partly united; the Tulip, whose three pistils are united into one; the Apple, in which the sepals are closely combined with the pistils. In short, the flowers are few in which some of these cohesions do not occur, often so far diguising the original type as to render its recognition a question of difficult solution. But, fortunately for the student, nature, in almost every instance, has left seams and marks to indicate the places of these abnormal unions.

Thus, in the briefest manner possible, we have glanced at the primeval type of the flowers, and alluded to the mazy dances of the floral tribes which cluster around her and follow closely in her train. We have seen how infinite diversity may be consistent with essential unity, and how a common principle may harmonize the widest apparent extremes.

Henceforth, we have the key to unlock the mysteries of this beautiful science, and a simple standard into which we may reduce all the vagaries of the floral structure, and so judge of their nature and character.—*California Teacher.*

RESIDENT EDITOR'S DEPARTMENT.

THE JOURNAL. Impaired health and a desire to become better acquainted with the educational systems and institutions of other countries may cause us to be absent for a few months and to relinquish the immediate oversight of two or three numbers of the Journal. It will be left in good and experienced hands, and will be ably edited and regularly issued in our absence. Contributors will please send their communications as now, directed to the " Editor of the Common School Journal, New Britain." Teachers, School Visitors, and other friends of education are invited to furnish local items of general educational interest.

We have in the present number an excellent article from a former contributor whom we gladly welcome again to our pages. We also commend the article on " Cultivation of Taste and Ornamentation," by Prof. Bail, to the careful study of teachers and parents. We hope to see our common schools become nurseries for the cultivation of taste and a higher regard for true art.

NORMAL SCHOOL. THE LATE BOARD OF TRUSTEES. In taking leave of the Normal School, justice requires that we should bear our testimony to the fidelity of those who so long watched over the interests of this institution. The Board of Trustees for sixteen years had the Normal School under their care. Our official relations with some of the members of the Board extended over a period of more than fifteen years. These were years of trial, of change, but of importance to an institution just called into life, founded for a specific object, and yet to be conducted without any long-tried precedents or established principles to guide it.

The Board was composed of men representing different political parties, religious persuasions, and professional and business vocations. Yet their deliberations were harmonious, and their efforts for the success of the school and the advancement of the cause of popular education were united and constant. All the members of the Board had been connected with local boards of school visitors in the different counties, and all had been identified with the common schools of the State. They were well acquainted with the wants of these schools, and understood how these wants were to be supplied. Nearly all had been members of both branches of the Legislature, and from their public and private relations had unusual opportunities of knowing the sentiment of the people of the State in relation to education. A committee consisting of two or three members of the Board visited the Normal School each term, examined the classes and methods of instruction, and once at least every year, the whole Board met at the school and devoted several days to an examination of its work. The faithful examinations, judicious criticisms, and the kind words of encouragement of different members of the Board, will long be remembered by all who have ever taught or studied in the Normal School. For their faithfulness, their wise counsel, and their continued efforts, they have been entitled to, and we believe have received, the gratitude of the true friends of the Normal School, and of all who desire the real advancement of the schools of the state.

The Normal School and the cause of education have also been much indebted to Gov. Buckingham for the constant support he has given them through the whole of his administration.

The State Board of Education, which now has charge of the Normal School, has signified its interest in the institution and its intention to re-organize it. We trust that this Board may receive the co-operation of the friends of education, and so plan for the school as shall increase its efficiency and make it still more a blessing to the common schools of the State.

NORMAL SCHOOL FOR FREEDMEN. At the last annual meeting of the American Institute of Instruction, in New Haven, Mr. E. Bassett of Philadelphia spoke in behalf of the education of the Freedmen in the Southern States, and advocated that as soon as possible, teachers should be educated from his own race.

Mr. Bassett is himself a graduate of the Conn. Normal School, and the respect he has secured in his position as principal of the Collegiate Institute for colored youth, Philadelphia, is an argument in favor of the cause he advocated so eloquently at New Haven.

Mr. Mortimer Warren, formerly of New Britain, and for the past year superintendent of the schools for freedmen in New Orleans, has just organized a school in that city for the training of colored teachers. The school is for the present in one of the Grammar school buildings.

It is composed of scholars (colored) selected from the higher departments of the city schools. The building occupied is convenient for the school at present. Blackboards and text-books have been secured,—the latter furnished by government, we think; but reference books and other accessories are much needed. Mr. Warren is a graduate of our State Normal School, an earnest Christian teacher who has been very successful in this state, and he will, we believe, succeed in his present benevolent enterprise. He is enthusiastic and hopeful in it, and we trust he may have an opportunity to develop his plans and accomplish the work he has undertaken.

REPORTS.

Twenty-first Annual Report of the Board of Trustees of the Public Schools of the City of Washington. This pamphlet contains the report of the Special Committee on Annual Report, with reports of the Committees on Text-books, Teachers' Institute, Examination of Teachers, Vocal Music, &c.

The whole number of pupils enrolled during the year was 5,883. The number on the register January 1st, 1866, was 4,139. There are 8 Grammar Schools, 8 Intermediate Schools, 28 Secondary Schools, and 28 Primary Schools; aggregate, 72 schools with 72 teachers. The average daily attendance was 48 to each school, or 3,456 in all the schools. The course of study for the Grammar Schools includes some branches usually pursued in High Schools, such as Ancient Geography, Astronomy, Geometry, Algebra, and Mental Philosophy. A copy of Webster's Unabridged Dictionary has been placed in each Grammar School.

PENNSYLVANIA. *Report of the Superintendent of Common Schools.* We have received from Hon. Chas. R. Coburn, State Superintendent of Penn., his report for 1865.

From this report, we learn that aside from the city and county of Philadelphia, there were in 1865, 1,837 school districts, with 12,548 schools, and 629,587 pupils in attendance. The average attendance was a little less than sixty-three per cent., and the average length of school term five months and fourteen days. The average cost of each pupil per month, including all expenses, was sixty-eight cents. Whole number of teachers, 14,286; average salary of male teachers per month, $31.82; of female teachers, $24.21.

In the city and county of Philadelphia, there were two High Schools, sixty-one Grammar Schools, seventy Secondary Schools, one hundred and ninety Primary Schools, and fifty-three classified schools, or an aggregate of three hundred seventy-six free schools, in which there were employed 84 male teachers and 1,194 female teachers.

Three of the twelve Normal School Districts into which the State is now divided are now supplied with Normal Schools. These schools are all prosperous. The county superintendents frequently allude to the benefits already derived from them.

WISCONSIN. *Seventeenth Annual Report of the Superintendent of Public Instruction,* by Hon. John G. McMynn. We published a portion of the statistics found in this report in the last number of the Journal. School-houses are improving, but much money is wasted by building without any suitable plan. Some of the school-houses are well provided with maps, charts, pictures, school apparatus, and in some instances the aisles are carpeted. The Superintendent recommends the founding of a State Industrial University, and suggests the plan recommended by Prof. John A. Porter of Yale Scientific School, New Haven.

LOCAL AND PERSONAL.

NORTH STONINGTON. There are residing in this town upwards of one hundred persons that have been or are now engaged in teaching. During the autumn months each year there are select schools maintained in different parts of the town, where many of our young men and misses are advanced to such a degree as to consider themselves qualified to teach.

Though North Stonington is well represented with teachers worthy the name, yet I am led to think if they had attended a Normal School the advantage to them and their success would have been greater. We are not able to retain our best teachers in our schools, for there is scarcely a district in town which is willing to give them a compensation which they readily command elsewhere.—*Extracts from Letter of S. A. Babcock, A. S. V.*

WATERBURY. YOUNG LADIES' COLLEGIATE INSTITUTE. The building for this institution is now completed, and it is among the finest for school purposes in the State.

The main building is 54 feet by 49, with a wing on the east end 68 by 30, and another on the west of 14 feet, giving a front view of 131 feet. The tower over the portico rises to the height of 71 feet. From this tower a fine view of the city and surrounding hills can be had.

The first floor contains a large double parlor, sitting-room, dining-room, kitchen, store-rooms, &c., in the main building, with school-rooms, recitation-rooms, and anterooms for scholars in the wing. There are also music-rooms in this story. The second story is mostly appropriated to sleeping-rooms, while in the third story are additional lodging-rooms and a spacious gymnasium. The building is heated by steam, is well ventilated, and supplied with gas, water, baths, &c.

The Institute has three distinct departments—the Elementary, the Academic, and the Collegiate. Each department is supplied with competent teachers, and the whole work is under the charge of Rev. R. G. Williams and Mrs. M. E. Williams, Principals. Lectures are given each term by gentlemen from abroad. We hope this school will be liberally sustained.

CONTENTS—MAY.

Cultivation of Taste,	129
Know Your Scholars,	134
Phonic Reading,	140
Doctrine of the Typical Flower,	144
Resident Editor's Department,	149
Reports,	151
Local and Personal,	152

Printed by Libri Plureos GmbH in Hamburg, Germany